Alone *yet* *not* Alone

Discovering God's
Healing Presence
in Whatever
Struggle
You Face

by Oscar Twikala

First Edition

Cover design/interior design/editing: Dana Susan Beasley | AngelArts.biz

ISBN: 978-0-578-65741-7

Cover picture: Bekleyiş | Adobe Stock © The Cheroke #184886212

Scripture quoted by:

The Holy Bible, English Standard Version. ESV® Text Edition: 2016. Copyright © 2001 by Crossway Bibles, a publishing ministry of Good News Publishers.

NEW AMERICAN STANDARD BIBLE®
Copyright © 1960, 1962, 1963, 1968, 1971, 1972, 1973, 1975, 1977, 1995 by
THE LOCKMAN FOUNDATION
A Corporation Not for Profit
LA HABRA, CA
All Rights Reserved
http://www.lockman.org

The Holy Bible, New International Version® NIV®
Copyright © 1973, 1978, 1984, 2011 by Biblica, Inc.®
Used by Permission of Biblica, Inc.® All rights reserved worldwide.

Printed in the United States of America.

Dedication

———◇———

*M*y heart goes out to people who are facing a difficult time, whether it's divorce, the loss of a loved one, facing a trial, false accusations, or injustice. When I was writing this book, I was thinking of you. I am thinking about those who are trying to voice their opinions, but they are not heard.

This book goes out to those who need someone to listen to them and somebody who understands them. To people who are facing depression and anxiety and have tried everything humanly speaking, but nothing worked. I just want to say that I am with you and this book is dedicated to you.

I dedicate this book to all my friends for their support. To all my mentees and my church. I dedicate this book to my previous boss's boss for all her boldness and candid feedback, and for such great professional development that she offered me. To my dear assistant for always being there when needed and motivating me when I didn't feel like working. To my manager and all my team who are supporting this ministry. To my father for always being there and for always supporting me and giving me so much love. To my mother for always believing in me and supporting me. She's always that "extra push" for me to go forward and I love her dearly. To my Pastor for all his prayers and words of encouragement.

Finally, to the Only Person who was there that night when I needed someone to talk to, I dedicate this book.

Table of Contents

Forward

I met Oscar Twikala several years ago at the intersection of my company's need for bilingual skills and his talent with people and languages. To make a very long story short, we began hiring people from Congo who were not yet fluent in English. Oscar was a skilled translator, and he quickly became a favorite resource for us.

But his talent ran far deeper than his skill with languages, expert that he was. His real talent was his ability to be the bridge between people and their needs. Or to go even further, his unshakable desire to be that bridge.

If you have had the pleasure of getting to know Oscar, then, like me, you may have first noticed his mild disposition and easy smile—just a frank friendliness that makes him easy to be around. Before long, you will have noticed that he puts great effort and energy into helping others.

I'm guessing that's where his urge to write begins. He speaks to what he knows. And he knows intuitively that we share certain tendencies, behaviors, and certainly fears. That must be where the topic of "alone" originates. The sense of aloneness is universal, and this book shows that Oscar has found a way to make peace with that—and we all can, as well.

Loneliness as a topic has been tackled by countless poets, essayists, and novelists. Oscar brings to the discussion the details of his own internal struggle and his ability to reason through it. His book is worth reading to get to his final assessment—that being alone can actually be a source of comfort and peace.

If this book brings you a bit of peace, I am sure that Oscar will count all his efforts as worthwhile.

—Suzy Parn
Retired Director of Personnel

by Oscar Twikala

Introduction

One of the big fear factors for every human being—and some may argue that saying every human being is an exaggeration—is the fear of being alone. Even our pets feel it when we are gone too long. No one enjoys being alone.

But is it possible for those of us who have big families or who are married or who have many friends—even people with millions of fans—to fear being alone? No one enjoys that. The fear of being alone will sometimes take us to a place of desperation where we worry that people in our lives will leave us. When they give us signs that they want to leave, we will try everything to keep them. Some of us will even try to buy friendship or any kind of a relationship because of the fear of being alone.

We get upset when people reject us, and we will try to manipulate them to stay with us. Then, when we find ourselves rejected and alone, we may become anxious because we do not want to face our feelings of loneliness.

Is it really such a terrible thing to be alone? That is the question I am asking. My hope is that through this book, we all will discover if it is only an emotional stage or a fact that we really are alone. Is there even such a thing as being alone?

I have always been a person who has sought for people to be around me and sought relationships. Some have worked and been successful and some have been unbelievably bad experiences. I grew up in a family where I was not living with my mother, but lived with my father and stepmother. My father was gone traveling all the time, so I was left at home alone with my stepmother. You can imagine the insecurity, fear, confusion, and isolation I felt because I did not have a voice. I felt the absence of both my parents and I did not get much attention from them. This was not intentional but based on circumstances. I turned to others for the attention that I did not receive from my parents. At the time, I felt so lonely and suffered from depression.

In this book, I will use my own experiences of being alone and feeling lonely and also the experiences and stories of others who have been alone—such as those who have been in the hospital by themselves, or facing a difficult time without any support from family or friends, or those who are alone in prison because of their own mistakes, poor choices, or poor judgment or because of injustice. I will talk about being alone and how I overcame the feeling of loneliness.

On a particularly long and challenging day, I was overwhelmed because I had a lot going on and there were too many things on my mind. All day long I had hoped to find someone with whom I could share my reality—someone to talk to—yet there was no one. Since I never found anyone to talk to, I decided to take a break from everything that night and I went running to clear my mind. When I was running that night, I received the insight from God to talk about loneliness. In that moment, I had to admit something and just accept that there was no one else around me. The question was—what was I going to do about it?

by Oscar Twikala

Through this book, I am going to share everything that I learned in that moment and how I came through that stage of loneliness. My hope is that this book may encourage you who have lost a partner, a friend, or a family member. Maybe you feel that you are rejected and looked down upon, and you feel that nobody cares about you or pays attention to you. I hope that every word and sentence in this book lifts you up and gives you the courage to move forward and to know that you're not alone. It is just how you see it, and perhaps it could all be in your mind.

by Oscar Twikala

Chapter 1: Fear

―――――◆―――――

Fear is the feeling that we all have when we are facing a tough time alone. We will seek a hand, a person—someone to be there for us and with us who will make things easier. I have heard people asking, *"Who will be there when I become old and weak? Who is going to be there and hold my hands and support me?"*

These questions that we ask ourselves cause so much tension and can lead to depression. We wonder what the future holds for us. Yet there are underlying worries we have that are within our fear of the unknown future. For example, one of those fears is being left alone when we lose our husband or wife prematurely and unexpectedly. Another thing we dread is facing judgment or failure by ourselves, so we seek that presence of another human being who can support us as we go through those difficult times.

A lot of people worry about what the future will look like. We are anxious by what the future holds for our children—the next generation—and the challenges that they will face. We are distressed about what nature will look like for them—based on current climate changes—which many believe is caused by the impact we have had on the natural world around us. Many people fear that there is *"an increase in the atmospheric concentrations of greenhouse gases [which] produces a positive climate forcing, or warming effect. From 1990 to 2015, the total warming effect from green-*

*house gases added by humans to the Earth's atmosphere increased by 37 percent"** This terrifies many people.

We are afraid of things that we can control and things that we cannot control. There is a fear that we call "what if." A lot of times, people are wrong to have this all-consuming worry. The fear of "what if" is a probability or possibility that something bad might happen, yet it may not happen. That fear is of something we cannot control.

I know of a man who had that panicked feeling of "what if." In high school, he feared what his life would be like if he didn't get his diploma. He had those thoughts because he struggled in school, yet he finished high school and even went on to college. Then in college, he was alarmed that he would not be able to finish college and get his degree. Yet, when he finished college and got a new job, he was fearful that he would lose his job. If that happened, then he worried about having enough income to get married. When he got married, he was scared by the thought of losing his wife. Once he and his wife had kids, he became apprehensive that he could also lose his kids. So, at every stage in this man's life, there were always those what-if questions troubling his mind: *What if I don't have this or that? What if this doesn't work out? What if I lose that? What if this part of my life doesn't move forward?*

We have all had those kinds of thoughts and fears. This

EPA.gov; "Climate Change Indicators: Greenhouse Gases"; Article from the EPA.gov website was read and saved on 7:29PM on 11.19.2019. https://www.epa.gov/climate-indicators/greenhouse-gases; Article "Climate Change Indicators: Greenhouse Gases").

man's life is an example to bring to light in our minds all these fears we share. *What if my friends don't like me anymore? What if people discover something scandalous about me that I don't want anyone to know?* We all have those thoughts. What we don't realize is that those "what ifs" are what we cannot control. Why would you fear something that you are not even sure will ever happen? That element right there is the very thing that will bring anxiety and depression. It is this terrifying "what if." We have a choice to hold onto something that is real; but, most of the time we choose the one that is not real.

On the other hand, some what-if fears are halfway true. Maybe we worry, *what if I die?* It is inevitable that we will all die, and it can happen to us at any time. Whether we are sick or healthy, there is still that what if. We can take the best care of ourselves by eating healthy and exercising and managing stress, yet we can still die prematurely of a heart attack—perhaps with no warning signs. On the other hand, I know of people who are not conscientious about their health, and, for example, may eat fast food for years without any problems with high cholesterol or high blood pressure. I am not trying to discourage us from being healthy. I am just pointing out that we worry about our own deaths when we ultimately have no control over it.

Another "what if" we fear is the loss of our jobs. There is the possibility that any one of us could lose our jobs, whether we are good at our jobs or not. We worry about the possibility of getting fired. Maybe the company you work for must downsize and your department is the one that gets shut down and you find yourself without a job and having to start all over again with a new company. Some of us have been forced to get training or take courses to find a new career entirely. We are afraid of this happening to us because we know people who have gone through this. There have been many great companies that were once strong and successful employers for hundreds or thousands of hard-working people and then one day, out of the blue, they go bankrupt. Then, all of a sudden, you find yourself feeling helpless and angry because you may have invested 20 years of your life to that company and then suddenly it closes its doors and you don't know how you will provide for your family.

Yes, these are frightening thoughts that may keep people awake at night. We know of people who get laid off and cannot find work and end up losing their homes or end up getting divorced because of the stress on their marriage. We know of people who get laid off and cannot find work. Yes, it can happen, so we live with the anxiety of what if it does. Some of us will end up just carrying that what-if fear throughout our whole 40-year career and it will never happen. For some of us, we will make it to retirement and then start worrying about other things. *What if our pensions are jeopardized because the commercial banks that manage our retirement funds could collapse?* We read the news every day and see an overwhelming number of things to worry about and to fear, yet worrying about these "what ifs" will not affect the unforeseen future. We're not going to do ourselves any good by worrying about it because we don't know what will happen.

Some of us will even go to our graves still worrying what will happen after we're gone. We will still worry about our retirement money and if we'll still have it. *What's going*

*to happen when I am gone and who's going to get my money?
We worry, "Will my son finish college, because I was the one
who was pushing him through it? What's going to happen?"*

We worry about everything and nothing. We worry
about what's going to happen, even though we're not
around. Why would you worry when you're not going to be
there? Yes, these concerns can be valid, and it is all right to
plan. What I am saying is do not waste your time worrying
about these things because we'll be gone, and we won't
know what will happen in the future.

There are things that we have absolutely no control
over. Yes, I understand some of these things are possible
and some are inevitable. There are people who go to the
doctor and he tells them that they have only three months
to live. There are people who will live longer than three
months. There are people who were given that prognosis
who will even live for years beyond those three months.
They were going along living their lives, but in that moment
when the doctor declares they have three months to live,
then they are worried. The point that I am saying is that we
are wasting our time worrying about things that we cannot
control. We do not know whether we have three more days
or 30 more years to live. So, how can we possibly live our
lives to the fullest, if we are paralyzed by the fear of death?

So, that fear of what-if can be true. However, sometimes, it's wrong, such as in the case of the man I previously
mentioned whose obsessive fears never came true. Still, he
worried at every stage of his life about the worst-case sce-
nario. I myself used to be in those shoes. I used to have a
fear of the future and of all the negative things that could
happen. I wasted a lot of time thinking about anything and

everything that could possibly go wrong in the future. A lot of times that's what we all do. We train ourselves to believe that something bad might happen tomorrow and we build our trust in those negative things that could happen tomorrow, while being unable to focus on the present.

What we forget is that when we worry about the "what if," we are, in fact, negatively affecting our health. And when we do that, the very same thing that we are afraid will happen we allow it to happen. So, *you may ask me how can I not worry? There's so much going on with my job, with my marriage, with college and university, about our children and their college and how their lives will turn out and with this and that.* You can come up with a whole list of things that are not working.

But the question that I am going to ask you is the very same question that Jesus asked in Matthew Chapter 6, *"By your worry, what are you changing in your life?"* Jesus went on to say if you worry, you are not going to add an hour to your life or change your hair to become whiter or darker. It is not going to change anything. Yet, you worry, and He said, *"Do not worry."*

Trust me, I understand. You may be experiencing a lot of tension and you may be experiencing a lot of difficulties. But here's one thing you can do about fear: You must rebuke it because it's the most dangerous enemy that you have within you. It's fighting you little by little, and surely, it's taking you down. Here is the advice that I am going to leave you with: Jesus said, *"Live each day today and do not worry about tomorrow. Let tomorrow take care of itself."*

I just want to point out that fear comes through a lot of things. Sometimes, it can be coming from what we have seen, like a parent maybe failing, or a brother or a family member or someone we were looking up to. So, seeing that person failing becomes a threat to us and we start thinking that because they failed, we may fail, too, so it brings fear into our lives. Because a lot of people just have a fear to try. They have a project but they never start. For some of us, maybe it is to write a book, or to accomplish something on our bucket list. But there's this great fear that takes control of us so we never try. A lot of people left us. They passed away with a lot of unfinished projects—a lot of things they wanted to do and to accomplish—but they never tried. Why? Because of fear. So, fear became the greatest enemy to them. It can be for us, too. That's why in the Book of Isaiah 54 the Bible says rebuke fear. Fear is something that we must rebuke. We have to deal with it.

It can stop you from living what God has planned for you: a life of joy. Here, I'm talking about joy that this world can't give to us. The greatest blessing that we can ever have only comes from Christ and through Him. But, again, fear is a threat to us. That's why I said before: Jesus commanded us not to fear. The Bible tells us to rebuke it. Fear must not come near us, says the Book of Isaiah. So, it's something that we need to deal with seriously. Attack it.

So, how do I get out of the grip of fear? If I have a fear to write a book, then maybe it's because I'm afraid of what people will think and what people will say. Well, I'll go ahead and write it. If I have a fear of speaking in front of people, then I'll just go ahead and do it. I don't know what you are afraid of. The only way to get beyond fear is to break that barrier. Believe me, with my first book, I had fears because this was a new experience for me, and I feared what people would think and what if people didn't like it? And then, I'm like: *"Well, anyway, I am not doing it for me. It's not about me. It's not about making me feel good, you know."* So, I started thinking about the right reason for writing this book. And when I took myself out of the equation, the fear was gone.

Chapter 2: Would You Listen?

A lot of times what people want is just to talk to someone or to find someone who will listen to them. Really, it is hard to find someone who is willing to listen. I have found myself often being prompted to give advice to others and showing others how they should do things. Let's be honest; we all do that, right? But do you ever wonder if the person talking to you doesn't need any advice from you, although you are wise and intelligent? Have you ever wondered if all we really want is someone who will listen?

I have come to realize that when I was in the position of receiving advice from someone, a few of those times in my life, I just wanted to talk and just needed someone to listen and not say a word, although it is in our nature that we are talkers and not listeners. If only we could listen, wouldn't that make a significant difference in our relationships?

Growing up, I had a lot of things to say but I was not so willing to listen. Would you say that the mistakes that you made when you were a teenager was because your father or your mother never talked to you? Would you say that the reason you lost that job was because during your training or your orientation nobody said anything to you? The real question is whether we are really listening to others. Are we listeners?

In this chapter, I am not here to give a lesson on how to

become an active listener, but just to remind us that not every person who comes to you and starts talking to you wants to hear what we have to say. Really, all they want is for you to listen to them. I am talking about your friends who are frustrated because they have so much going on in their hearts and in their minds. When they are talking to you, you think, *what they are saying doesn't even make sense!* It's because the heart and the mind are talking at the same time. It doesn't matter if their thoughts flow correctly or whether what they are trying to say makes sense. They just want you to listen.

Also, I am talking here about people who have never been heard, but they have so much to say. I am talking about the teenager who is trying to say something, but his parents are so right that they cannot even listen to him. The minute this teenager tries to say a word, his parents cut him off by telling him that he is not even making sense. You're not going to understand the feeling of not being heard if you have never been in that position.

Oftentimes, you'll have someone having that burden in their chest who is just trying to find a place to release it; and yet, there is no one willing to listen. When she's a friend, she says, *"Hey, Man, you don't make sense."* When he's a husband, she says, *"You need to talk to someone. Your head is not right."* Really, many people are wanting to talk to doctors, psychiatrists, psychologists, and counselors not because they are losing their minds, but because the people in their lives won't listen to them. So they are referred to people who are paid to be good listeners.

Is it really that your daughter wants to pay someone to listen to her, or that your wife wants to go and sit in session for an hour with someone she pays to listen to her? Some people will even go to the bar and sit for hours telling the bartender things about their families and themselves and their problems just because at home they have no one to listen to them.

I was only 18 when I gave my first counseling session. Trust me, I am not saying that I was an expert, but I was just willing to listen. I would sit for hours with this old lady and she would tell me about her kids, brothers, and sisters. She would tell me everything and nothing. I think it would be easy for me to write the story of her life, but I am not going to do it. Here's the point: if you can listen, then I certify you as a counselor.

One day, as I was walking down the street, I saw a man sitting on a bench. I don't know if he was an angel or not, but what he told me impacted my life even until today. As we were talking together, this man asked me if I liked poetry, and I said yes, *"I love writing and I love poetry."* Then, he gave me his method of writing poetry which he called *"Look, Listen, and Observe."* I will never forget that. As we were talking, I would speak to him and try to tell him things and show him that I was smart, and he would just stop me and say, *"Look, Listen, and Observe."* That is all I needed.

Many times, we rush to speak and to prove our point. We want to be right; we want to be correct, and we want to be smart. No one is willing to do these three things: look, listen, and observe. Trust me, they all go together.

You might say your husband is insane, and your wife is losing it, and your kids are crazy. But really, take a minute and look at them. Are they truly insane, crazy, and losing it? I know some of you will answer these questions with *"Yep,"* but let's be serious for a minute. Let's take time to look at them. Observe them. Observe your friend. Observe your boss. Observe the people around you and listen. No, I am not talking about hearing, because you can hear them all day long and what you hear is some crazy kid or a husband who is insane or a wife who is about to lose it, but can you just listen to their hearts? It is only by listening that we can get to the root of the problem. How would you understand someone just by the first sentence?

A lot of times, when we see people on the streets begging for money, it is easy for us to assume that all they need is money. That is not always true. I have encountered some homeless people who have only wanted someone to listen to them. It is easy for us to get caught up in thinking that *"Oh, they need clothes,"* so we buy them clothes. Or *"All these orphans need is to go to school,"* but we all can be wrong. Maybe they are searching for love, attention, or someone to listen to them.

Many homeless people have stories to share, but we don't have time to hear them. We judge them, saying, *"Oh, they have made poor decisions, so now they are on the streets"* or *"They had a lot of debt, which is why they are now living on the streets."* We don't know why they are there. For some homeless people, others have stolen their money. Maybe, for the majority, they are on the streets because of their poor decisions or the things they have done. There are so many reasons people find themselves on the streets. But, would you agree with me that everybody needs to be heard, even if they're wrong? Don't they also have the right to explain themselves to have someone hear what they have to say, even if they just want to say they are sorry? Perhaps they just want to ask or beg for forgiveness.

One time as I was doing my laundry I met a homeless lady. Other than giving her money, I gave her my ears. She started talking about herself and her past. As she was telling her story, I could see that she didn't have anyone who would sit with her and let her share her heart. While she was sharing, she had tears running down her face. I didn't say a word. I just sat with her and she talked for some time and that was it. I could tell that she was carrying a burden and was just looking for a place to go release it. My point is that you may be the person that someone is asking for. You may be the psychiatrist that someone is looking for. That person who wants to speak to you may be your friend, brother, sister, mother, or father. Perhaps, your husband or wife wants to speak to you. They want you to listen to them. I am not talking about hearing—because you have been hearing them for a long time. They want you to listen to their hearts.

It can be very frustrating when no one is listening to you. I remember a story that my mother shared with me about a time when she went to see her doctor. She was trying to explain what was going on to her doctor, but he was using his experience as a doctor to come to his own conclusions without listening to her. It was terribly disappointing for her, so we would pray that she would find a new somebody who was willing to listen to her. My mom was frustrated because her own doctor didn't listen to her.

I myself have been in those shoes of not being able to listen. One of my friends, after failing her exam in nursing school, was so discouraged. She was in pain. She was looking for someone to listen. I did a good job for a few weeks. As she would talk, I would sit and listen. After that, she would feel relief and she would be fine. Then, she would come back again. Her emotions would change all the time. She'd be fine for a while. Sometimes she'd be happy and sometimes she'd be sad. It was normal because of what she was experiencing—after failing her nursing board exams. I was doing a good job just being a listener. She didn't want me to give her advice or counseling. She just wanted someone to understand.

Because I knew that was what she wanted. Things between us were going just fine, until I gave her a piece of advice. I told her, *"You have been complaining for weeks and you're wasting your energy."* I told her to look forward and to move forward. Whatever I told her was the truth, but she didn't want it. She just wanted me to listen. We were no longer on the same page and she got frustrated with me now, because I told her to move on. She didn't want my smart advice. She just wanted me to listen.

So, in this case, what do you need to do? Give people more time to heal. Give them time to heal and they will get there, but they need time to speak about whatever is in their hearts. When they need your advice, they will ask you the simple question, *"What do you think?"* That's when you can speak up and tell them, *"Hey, you need to move on."* If they haven't asked that, then don't go ahead and tell them what you think. If it's something that they want, they will let you know.

That was a valuable lesson I learned that day, and I think it can be valuable for you, too. Take time to listen to the people who are talking to you. Don't be prompt to tell them what you think. Just listen to them.

Let's think about how we talk to teenagers. Do we know how to listen to them? We like to say, *"I was a teenager once."* But if you were a teenager in the 1980s, then you are talking about a different time. In the '80s, we didn't have the same challenges that teens have today. There were no smartphones. There was no Internet or social media. It's much more complicated and challenging for teenagers and children now.

Talking in a kid's language is something different than talking in your language. Maybe you'll say, *"I used to be a kid, too,"* or *"I used to be a teenager"* but your time and her time are different. The world has changed. Some things in the human condition remain constant, I know, but still we have differences.

So, how can you understand this kid? Just listen to her. A lot of times, we cannot listen because we don't have time and we want it to be quick and for her to tell us things right away and get to the point. Maybe they don't want to get to the point and they just want us to listen to their hearts, and not just their minds.

This can relate to all kinds of relationships: just take time to hear the person and understand the heart. Give them time to speak about their frustrations, their feelings on something that has happened to them inside their world, and how it is affecting them, because into the heart of a man is a profound river that only God can reach.

However, you have sweet people who know how to touch the surface of that subconscious place. Therefore, a genuine word of encouragement and gesture of love can have a deep impact on someone's spiritual wellbeing. All it takes is for you to tell this person, *"I hear you and I am listening to you."* Even though for now it doesn't make sense in your mind, just take in all the information that this person is saying.

I know a lot of times we will say this person is self-centered, but the only way we can help them out of themselves is to listen to them because we may not understand where their behaviors are coming from. We need to understand where their behaviors are coming from in order to help them. Willingness to listen allows us to go to the root of that problem.

There are a lot of people who just need somebody to listen to them. You can practice that with anyone. Try to work on it with your family. Sit down and don't say a word and just listen to your kids. If you feel like you want to say something, ask them, *"Do you want to hear my opinion on the subject?"* but just practice listening. Maybe you are a pastor and there are people out there in your congregation who just want you to listen them. Practice it. Practice with your friends at work. Just sit there and let the information sink in and just listen. Don't say a word. If you feel like you *want to say something, then ask the person, "Do you want to hear my opinion or what I think?"* Sometimes, they will ask you what you think, and you can say what you think. If they do not, then just listen. If you can listen, then I certify you to be a counselor.

Remember in the introduction of this book, I said that there was a specific time that I was looking for somebody to listen to me. It was not because I couldn't find anybody to listen to me. It was because some people were busy or some were not there or some thought that whatever I said didn't make sense to them, so they were like, goodbye. I was looking and seeking somebody to listen to me. I had to admit something that night—that I was alone, and there was nobody to listen to me. So, as I was walking, I could speak to God. He was there, listening to me, and not questioning me. He didn't say a word. He just listened and it was perfect!

I told Him everything. I shared my frustrations, and I let my heart speak out loud and I told Him everything and I withheld nothing. He didn't say a word and it worked. I felt relief that night. Then, He told me to *go tell somebody that if he needs someone to talk to and to listen, then I am here. I'm an expert. I won't say a word. I'm just going to listen.* That's the key. Don't look left and right to try to find an expert. They'll always have something to say.

I am not discouraging anybody from going to see a professional who will listen to them. I am saying that if you need somebody to just listen to you and not give you advice, then talk to God. It can be for hours with Him. It can be for days. It can be for years. The Bible says in the Book of Exodus Israel was talking and talking to God for 400 years, and He didn't say a word. He was silent until they asked Him, *"What do You say?"* so then He told them. If you want to know what God is thinking about a particular situation just ask. But if you want someone to listen, He can do that for as long of a time as you need Him.

Chapter 3: Pain

———————◇———————

*P*ain—is it really a bad thing? Most people will answer this question with a yes, but here is what I am asking you to do: Would you think for a little bit? I will give you just a few examples of pain that later on down the road became a blessing.

One good example that I have for us is a woman who is giving birth. First, I want to mention that because I am a pastor many women have shared their experiences with having babies, and so I am telling about their experiences with all respect. Some women told me, *"Pastor, I wanted to punch my husband and I hated everybody, because it was so painful."* That process has never been an enjoyable thing for women. When it is happening to them, they weep, and they will pinch their husbands, and, during the worst of it, they will even punch their husbands and push their doctors. So, the process of childbirth is a very a painful experience, and if you ask these women if they want to stay there and keep doing what they are doing, you can imagine what they might say because they don't like it all.

But the minute she hears her baby crying in the room and she sees her baby for the first time, in that moment, she cannot really describe how beautiful it is. In that experience, she doesn't really have the words to explain or to express herself. But here's a question: How did that baby get here? Through pain.

Let me share another example: athletes. When they are training, it is a painful experience. I remember playing basketball in high school. During practice, we ran these drills that were called "suicides." (My readers who have played on a basketball team will know exactly what I am talking about.) It's a very painful experience and when my coach told me to do them, I didn't like it, but I wanted to play. And, in order to play well, I had to practice well.

Also, I can use the example of people who are studying to become nurses, doctors, or lawyers. I can go on and on and on, but if I focus just on the time of their studies, it was not an easy experience for them. They would push their minds and bodies to the absolute limits, which was difficult. Maybe they were not sleeping well, as they studied all night long for exams. It hurt them. They were tired. They were often at the point of exhaustion. Nevertheless, at the end of their studies and at the very moment they got their degrees, licensures, and certifications, then their pain was eased, and it became a blessing. Therefore, pain is not always a bad thing.

Sometimes, painful processes give us strength and wisdom. Through the process of pain, we also gain personal growth and knowledge. So, the pain that you have experienced becomes a blessing to you and to others. Something else we get through pain is discipline. We also develop self-control. We become humble. In the course of my life, I've come to realize that some of the painful experiences we go through are a blessing from God. God will allow you to go through that in order to give you character and to help you to look more like Him, and to walk and to speak like Him, but you get it through that painful experience.

Many people will ask, *"Well, isn't there any other way we can learn that, like a shortcut?"* A lot of people will ask for the shortcut through a difficult path. They want the short-cut.

Let's keep going with another example. Think about someone who has just signed up to join the military. Do you think you can just simply lecture him on how to become a soldier? No. Telling someone how to be a soldier does not make him a soldier. Talk to a veteran. If you ask any veteran, *"If you had to go back and do it all over again, would you want a shortcut through it?"* They would say no because the painful experience of their training was worth it.

There are some things you cannot learn sitting in a classroom. You have to practice. You have to be exposed to that environment, in order to be built up. So, soldiers don't know it during their training, but the minute they were out there fighting in the world, they realized that the painful experiences in training was worth it. It was vital and necessary.

Likewise, when the surgeon is training his residents in order to help them become self-controlled, calm, and disciplined, they don't like the pain of working for 36 hours straight without sleeping. They might say to themselves, *"This surgeon is against me! He doesn't like me!"* The residents will take it personally. Yet, by the time their residency is over, these new surgeons will have a different view of this veteran surgeon who trained them, and they will have a higher respect for him because of that experience.

Pain is not always a bad thing, but nobody wants it. A lot of men and women of character—trust me—they went through that process of pain. Maybe this is where you are right now, and you feel like you want to give up. If you were to go and ask everyone going through a painful experience, then they will tell you they want to give up also. This is what I want to tell you: don't give up.

Maybe you don't want to hear everything I am saying right now because you are in pain, and I understand that. But would you be open-minded? Would you be empathetic, in order to understand what I am talking about? I am going to explain one of my painful experiences. I have had many of them in the course of my life. Because of that, I believe that I can easily recognize someone in pain. It is easy for me to be patient with them and to love on them because I know the process. Because I was in that same spot of need-ing attention and love. But, trust me, I have gained a lot of experience and gifts through those painful struggles.

Maybe the pain you are experiencing right now is emo-tional or physical. It's all pain. Maybe you have experienced the painful loss of a loved one. Maybe you have suffered from the pain of injustice or the pain of trauma. I don't know. You name it because you know what you're suffering from. No matter what kind it is, pain is pain. Whether it is physical, psychological, or emotional, it's all pain, and trust me, we don't want it. I am empathetic and compassionate toward people in pain because I understand what they have been through.

I interviewed my good friend and coworker, Tammy Still, who shared with me her experience when she lost her husband. She said to me that it was hard, and the hardest part at the time was how she was going to tell her kids. They were so young, and they didn't understand what was going on. I mean, I can only imagine what she must have felt that day.

Tammy told me that her husband had gone on a fishing trip and the boat capsized. The river was narrow and extremely deep-fed from some mountains. Her husband got caught in an undercurrent. Tammy shared that it took a little more than 24 hours to find him and it was the worst 24 hours of her life, those long painful hours before they recovered his body. I cannot imagine the pain of waiting for his body to be found. I cannot grasp the pain that Tammy went through! It was a struggle—the not knowing—and then having to tell her five-year-old and three-year-old that their dad is gone. Although today she is remarried and has a happy family, Tammy told me that she is not sure that you can ever heal from losing somebody, but that you learn how to deal with the loss.

Tammy gave me permission to share about her pain. After her husband died, she went to live with her parents in her time of painful loss and mourning. She completely withdrew and stayed inside the house and had no interaction with the outside world because of the pain she was experiencing inside her. She told me, *"At the time that [my husband] passed, I physically hurt. My joints hurt. I didn't feel good, and there wasn't a day that I felt good, just from all the pain in my heart and in my head and in my soul."*

Tammy told me that it took her a long time to bury her husband. What she meant was that even though they had a funeral for her husband, and they had buried her husband, Tammy had not been able to let go of him. Tammy said that didn't change until the time she saw her husband. She said she saw her husband telling her that she had to move on, live her life, and let it go. That was the time when things changed for her. That's something personal and something we can't explain, but that was what happened to Tammy. As I mentioned earlier, Tammy didn't know what to tell her children about their father's death, but she told them that their dad had become an angel. At three and five, Tammy's children accepted that Dad had become an angel. Her kids would go around telling people, *"Dad became an angel! Dad became an angel!"* (I did so love that.)

So, Tammy looked for one thing every day that made her happy. For example, playing with her kids at the park or going out for ice cream. Sundays, Tammy and her kids went to church and Tammy found that it always made her feel better. She said that to overcome that grief and loss, she had to take those steps—one at a time—each day to help her move forward with her life. She said that she had to be motivated to take those steps. You have to want to be happy. Tammy said her greatest motivation was her children. She didn't want anyone else to raise them for her.

Trust me, I know this lady and she is one of the happiest people at work. Tammy doesn't care about a certain work policy because when she sees me, she always hugs me. She always smiles. She is upbeat. I have never seen her with a mean face. I never would have guessed that this tragedy was part of her story.

So, here I want to take a moment and talk to people who have lost a loved one. It can be your husband, your friend, or your brother. We always have words to tell those who are in sorrow. When we visit people who are grieving, we tell them, *"God gives and God takes away,"* but you wouldn't say that if it happened to you. Because I have been through the grieving process, when I visit someone who just lost a loved one, I tell them to cry. Cry as much as you can because it will bring healing. But I also tell them, *"Don't hang on to that. Let it go because it will kill you."*

I always tell grieving people one thing that has been a blessing to me. God may take someone we love from our lives, but He doesn't take everything. He takes the person but leaves us with our memories. So, I can go back in my memory and see all the great moments with that person. You don't have to think about the bad times when the person was yelling at you or throwing something at you. You can think of those great moments with that person. Maybe that time you shared a meal with that person or maybe the time you were taking a walk together or when you were hiking with this person who told you something very significant.

Take a moment and enjoy that memory. God didn't take that from us. I can be right here and close my eyes and be with my mother. I can also be with my biological father and hear every piece of advice that he gave me. So, I chose that path. We can choose to remember the good times and enjoy them and take that happy path, or we can take the path of sorrow and grief. I have taken the path of sorrow before, and believe me, it didn't help. That path will damage your health. It will damage you and cause you trouble so that you cannot enjoy your life. So, I can come here and give you all these things, because I have learned them through pain.

Remember that the work of God in us is a continual thing. Recently, I had been going through more painful experiences, and at the time, I didn't know what was about to happen. As I said in the chapter *Would You Listen?*, there was one day when I had wanted to share my struggles with somebody, but there was no one around. So, I told how I got the insight to write this book through my own pain. Now, I can see that God took my painful experience and turned it into a blessing to me. This is my hope for you: that God will bless all by reading this book. For all of you who are right now experiencing pain, I hope that God will take that pain and change it into a blessing for you and for the people in your life that you will touch and bless. That is something only God can do. He can take pain and turn it into a blessing.

I am going to share with you a poem that came to me through that painful experience, and maybe it will help you understand me. Here it is:

> *Oh Lord, the pain that I can't describe. I will test so that I may testify.*
> *I have been attacked by injustice, oh Lord, yet I will humble myself so that I may truly love.*
> *I feel lost by confusion, but I will face the darkness with courage so that I may shine through Your light!*
> *I will stop presenting and representing myself, so that You may speak on my behalf. Your Word is truth and Your judgment is righteous.*
> *Let all my days on earth and forever align with Your love, and I accept Your refuge. You know my heart, my love, my hope; it's for You. May I abide in You, so that I can stay away from destruction.*

So, this poem is coming through my pain. Now, I understand why David was writing down all the songs he had written. I can relate to that. That was David's pain, but it was an expression of worship to God. And, here in this poem, I am experiencing the same thing, and my pain also became an expression of worship to God. So, here I am experiencing the pain, but I did see God allowing me to go through it in order to grow. The minute I understood that this was an opportunity coming from the Lord, then that's why I said in the opening of my poem, *"Oh, Lord, the pain that I can't describe,"* but I am willing to take the test of pain. The testimony that I am giving you here came through that pain.

In the second verse, I said that *"I have been attacked by injustice, oh Lord, yet I will humble myself so that I may truly love."* So here, I am before the judge. I am before the Great Judge, God, and I am coming in front of Him, saying, *"I know that whatever is happening right now in my life, I can search and search and search, and I don't see anything wrong that I have done. I can see through the Light of Your Word what I have done wrong, yet right now I don't see it, and yet I have been attacked by injustice and false accusations. But, now, I am telling YOU that I will humble myself, true or not what people have said. It doesn't matter if it's false. I want to humble myself and I want to love like You love because You have been wrongfully accused. You didn't do it, but You humbled Yourself and You loved us."*

So, at that moment, I was telling God that I want to demonstrate His true love, and to love those who don't even deserve my love. I didn't deserve God's love in the first place. So here, my pain and what people were doing to me became an act of worship.

In the third verse, I wrote that *"I feel lost by confusion, but I will face the darkness with courage so that I may shine through Your light!"* With what was going on in that moment, I was feeling lost and in a place of confusion and darkness, but I was searching for the Light of God. I was searching for His Truth. I was searching for His Light so that I could shine. So, the Light of God that shines through us is a little bit like what the Sun does with the Moon. The Moon doesn't have its own light, but depends on the light of the Sun. When the Sun shines on the Moon, it can shine, too. The Sun is the source of the Moonlight. So, at that moment, I was looking for that Light of God, so that I could reflect God's Love so that it could shine in other people's lives. I was at a dark point, but God found me through His Love, and as an act of worship, I needed to put His Love on display. Trust me, it is not an easy thing to do, but it is our identity.

A lot of times when we feel accused by people, we will try to come up with the right words to explain ourselves and we will try to find people who will be on our side and who will convince others that we are bad people. Believe me, we will run from left to right to try to find people to defend us. So, we come in with the wrong defense attorneys. So, when those people trying to help us fail—and we fail to help ourselves—it starts to affect us negatively. We go through great stress and pressure that leads to severe depression and anxiety, and nothing helps to alleviate it.

So, in the fourth verse, at that moment, when I was trying to find someone who can defend me and represent me and present me, I was telling God that I find HIM to be the

Great Judge. He is the Righteous Judge whose judgments will not be corrupted, threatened, or swayed by others because His judgments are not based on feelings. He is not going to be emotional about anything, but He will be true. So, finally, I know that it is God who must present me and represent me, because I have been doing this for years and years and I am stuck here in the same place. I ask God to please speak on my behalf because His Words are true.

What I found very interesting is that in the Gospel, Jesus never presented or represented Himself. He was quiet and let the Father give the testimony. God spoke on His behalf. That is why Jesus' testimony is greater and more powerful, because God spoke on His behalf. So, understanding that, I wanted Him to present me and represent me, and the way God does that is through His Word, which is always truthful.

In the final stanza, after I had experienced God and His Love, I came to a time of decision. So, I said to Him, *"With what I know of You, I am praying for You to let all my days on Earth align with Your love."* I wanted to be more like Him. It can be possible but only through Him. So here I was surrendering myself to Him and I was abiding in Him. I was finding my refuge in Him because He is the only safe place.

A lot of times, we experience pain because we are out there, and we are outside, and we will not sit down and abide in Him. Many times, the Psalmist said to the Lord, *"I find my refuge in You,"* because he was out there and with no security for him. He was running away from Saul, because Saul could have destroyed him. He wanted to kill David.

There is a lot of destruction out there. The world can be very painful. It has become easier now for people to kill each other with no remorse. The world out there is evil. What we once called the moral standard doesn't exist anymore. So where can you find refuge? Some people will try through a relationship, but when it doesn't work, it hurts them. When they try through a friendship that doesn't work, then they end up being hurt again. I am not saying that relationships are bad, nor am I saying that friendship is bad. That is not what I am saying. What I am saying is that people are trying to find refuge in the things of this world, when our hope is in Him. Our hope is in God. Some people work and feel successful, but when they go home alone and go places by themselves, then they feel empty.

I have been in places where I have preached great sermons and God will use me in a very powerful way and people will say to me that they have been so blessed and say that was a great sermon, and then I will come home and I will feel empty. But when I abide in Him, then it doesn't matter what people think. It doesn't matter what people say. When I abide in Him, it doesn't matter if people try to hurt me. You must understand this. When God is in you, there will be times when people will try to put you down and slow you down and take you down. They did the same thing to Jesus. He was preaching the Truth and people were trying to take Him down and destroy Him. They tried to get Him to neglect His calling. They questioned what He was doing. Even when Jesus blessed people, they still questioned that.

So, listen, it doesn't matter what good you are trying to do or what gifts you are trying to give or in what ways you are trying to bless people. This is when people become frustrated. You are blessing people here and doing this and doing that and when it feels like people don't care, it hurts you. But Jesus wasn't preaching for people to acclaim Him and recognize Him. When the Pharisees would come and question Him, *"Under whose authority are you doing this and who gave you permission to heal on this day?"* Jesus didn't care what they said. Even when people called Him the devil—Beelzebub—Jesus was not hurt. Why? Because He was here to do His Father's business. Because He found His refuge in God. He abided in God. They were one; they were so united. They were so united that Jesus was disconnected from Earth. Because of that, Jesus would tell His people that our kingdom is not here. Our kingdom is in Heaven and our kingdom is to come. We are hurt because our hope is in the wrong things. We are to put our hope in the things from above. I wonder that if you really knew and understood the hope that you have of a home in Heaven, then what would hurt you here on Earth? Is it the promotion you didn't get or the relationship that you longed for was never meant to be? Or, is it that you are coveting my promotion and jealous of my relationship and that is hurting you?

What will hurt you? What could possibly hurt you knowing that if you die today—if you die right now—you'll be home?

Abide in God. Find rest in Him. Find peace in Him. Find hope in Him and find your home in Him.

Chapter 4: Many Around Me Yet Alone

We all have that moment. Whether you have a big family, or you have a lot of fans, or you have a lot of people believing in you, you can then experience that moment when you feel like the whole world has abandoned you. It happens, maybe not to you but to so many.

The Lord Jesus Christ, after having big crowds following Him and believing in Him, at the very moment at the Cross where He was executed, there was no one. Even though there were so many people around Him, in that moment of pain and suffering and death, He was alone. He was seeking for the hand of someone who would understand His experience and what He was going through.

To make that clear, when Jesus was in the Garden of Gethsemane, He was trying to get His disciples to understand Him. Because Christ knew what was about to happen, He asked them to pray with Him, but His disciples didn't understand Him and, they were, in fact, sleeping while He was in agony and praying by Himself. That experience was for Christ alone and no one else. So, to reinforce our case, even though He had His closest companions and beloved brothers with Him, He was alone. And, here I am talking about Jesus as a man because the pain, the betrayal, and the struggle were real, and He was seeking for that very hand, the Hand of God to touch Him.

There are many around us, yet we still feel alone. I know a story about this man of God. God used him to bless so many with his songs and preaching, but then, one day—one day, with one mistake—the whole world just crashed down on him. He said something that he wasn't supposed to say, and the flesh kicked in, and men were ready to stone him. I can only imagine the pain, the cry, and the struggle. Yes, at that place, what do we do? When you feel like everybody is against you—like no one understands you—what do we do at that moment?

I know most of us don't like that place. We are afraid to step out of our safe places and to go be in a crowd and just experience being by ourselves. I know many of you reading this are thinking that it hurts you to be in that situation, surrounded by a lot of people—like in a mall or crowded restaurant. It makes you uncomfortable to sit by yourself in those settings and then you believe you are a social outcast and you start feeling alone which causes you to experience the pain of loneliness. You cannot imagine how anyone would enjoy being alone by themselves with so many people around.

Here, I would like to share part of the interview I had with Suzy Parn, my boss's boss, for this book. I thought it was funny that Suzy actually likes going to crowded places, and just sitting there and experiencing it by herself. Suzy said that she doesn't experience loneliness the way others do. She also pointed out that being alone for long periods of time does not take her to the stage of loneliness because her mind remains active.

At the time of our interview, Suzy was getting ready to

retire and give up her busy career. I asked her whether she thought she would feel like there would be something missing in her life when she retired. Suzy agreed that people do wonder about that, but she indicated that she was optimistic and didn't anticipate that she would feel like anything is missing in her life. She said that she will remain involved in whatever she decides to do, such as picking up causes. She mentioned that in retirement, she hopes to do things that she has always wanted to, but never had time to do, such as raising chickens. Suzy said that she did not think there will be any holes in her life.

I told Suzy that there are many people out there who do struggle with loneliness and being in situations where they are alone, and I asked her what she would tell them. Suzy admits that she does not know what works for other people, but she shared what she hopes to do in retirement. She had a good career and aligned herself with the company and its values, which are good things. She devoted her life to working long hours for decades in the career she loves, but in retirement, Suzy intends to step away from everything for a while and give herself a chance to just sit and think. Also, Suzy wants to start writing and journaling again. In doing those things, Suzy hopes it will be a means for her to understand herself a little bit more and to understand what is driving her.

In terms of experiencing loneliness, Suzy stated that a lot is determined whether you are more of an introverted or extroverted person. She sees that there is a different dynamic that governs the two.

Suzy guesses that "introverts in general maybe would have less [or] fewer feelings of loneliness or aloneness because they tend to go deep into themselves…and they don't tend to need as much interaction in order to express themselves."

For extroverts, they express and understand themselves differently. Suzy had to learn how to be in a large group and have those kinds of conversations by watching other people. She said that the other part of that process is making a decision and being willing to go out there and make yourself vulnerable.

I went on to ask Suzy what she would tell someone who is wanting to be out there and wanting to connect, but they have been shut down, mocked, or bullied and how would she encourage someone willing to try but are just too afraid or shy to do that. Stating that this is an introverted person's answer, Suzy said for you to create a safe place for yourself but be aware of the dangers of going entirely inside that safe place to hide and to be a loner and not to interact with others because of the negative experiences and pain you've experienced on the outside. Suzy said that we need to have a small group of friends that we can trust implicitly who are our safe place, our anchor that provides "a foundation of safety" that allows us to go outside of ourselves and into big groups of people without fear.

So, like I was saying earlier, we all find ourselves in places where there will be a lot of people around us, yet we will still feel lonely. Those moments will be when we are at a funeral or if someone is facing a trial, for example. We have moments like that when we wonder what we can do at that particular moment.

I was once at a funeral with a grieving lady who lost her child who was her first-born. She carried that child for nine months (nine months!) hoping that when she delivered, she would finally have her baby. Normally, when a woman gives birth, there is a cry. There is a baby crying. But for some reason, at this lady's delivery, there was silence. She was shown—and here I am just trying to imagine—she was shown her baby was born, but there was only silence.

I went to the hospital to visit her and to encourage her, but believe me, I had no words. I didn't know what to tell her. I just encouraged her to cry and hoped that it would bring healing to her soul. And that was only the first part, but the second part was at the funeral. I was just trying to imagine her pain, but it was so hard to connect to it. I wanted to sympathize, but all that I felt was in the past, but she was living that struggle in that moment. So, as I sat down, I heard words coming to my ears and I started writing. I couldn't express well what I was feeling for her. I had my phone, and I opened my notes and started writing everything that came to my mind, and it became this poem that I am about to share with you:

She

I can only imagine, but she?
That melancholic music that takes you on a journey
*   into the desert, an eternity that nothing else can*
*   fulfill.*
Sad we all are, but she?
The imagination does not do enough work to bring
*   me into this deepest pain.*
Maybe some can meet her halfway so they can sym-
*   pathize, so they all have pain like her but it was*

in the past, but she?

Can you imagine the best gift you can give to your firstborn, but she?

God the Father had experienced the same thing when He saw His own Son mistreated on the cross.

He was able to do something but He decided to do nothing so that He could understand her.

In the deepest pain that plunged you into suffering that appears to be like eternity but the One who is eternal can fulfill that emptiness by the Holy Spirit.

There were so many hands but none of them could have kept her warm, but she?

In the cold and in the fear Jesus felt that moment of loneliness at the cross.

He shouted with a loud voice. He was searching for that Hand that would keep Him warm. Even His mother and every other woman and man who loved Him—all these hands—were unable to do anything for Him. God touched Him in the sepulcher where nobody could have reached Him and in a way that nobody could have imagined.

That very Hand she was also searching for through her tears.

The Holy Spirit, the Hand, the Power of the Living God was at the rendezvous.

That Hand was caressing her face and fulfilling her heart, but she?

I made this point in an earlier chapter: It is not a bad thing to be either introverted or extroverted. For me, I am both. It is not wrong to be in your own bubble, but the world is also around you. You have to still go out there and do things and make connections with people, even though you eventually have to go back into your little world. You just need to have a balance. It is a good thing to have your own moment if that is how you get restored.

That is fine, but you need to make sure that you come out because the world out there is still running.

Chapter 5: Alone

―――――◆―――――

I interviewed my friend who graciously shared her own struggles with loneliness and what she has learned from her experiences. Before sharing her own story, she made some valid points, saying that loneliness and being alone does affect people differently and that some people need to be surrounded by people, while others are perfectly content being alone. My friend said that she never knew loneliness while she was growing up in her parents' home. She became a mother at 19 and lived with her boyfriend and children. She was with the children 100 percent of the time, and once in a while would ask her boyfriend for much-needed alone time.

Recently, when my friend and her boyfriend separated, she was able to experience being alone. She had time to do things that she needed to do. For example, she could clean the house without having children running around. She learned how to be alone. She had time to go out and see movies by herself. However, at the end of some of those nights, my friend would realize that she struggled with feeling lonely. Yet she managed it by telling herself that one day she would find someone new.

My friend said that she was not afraid of being alone, but she said she was only afraid of ending up alone. But not at this point in her life. She has her children and is watching them grow up. She has her mom. Yet, she knows that her children will grow up and go lead lives of their own and that her mom won't be around forever. Knowing that one day everyone will either be gone or too busy for her is the scary part.

I asked her what she thought about lonely people doing desperate things in order to find someone to be with, such as spending money on people so that they will hang out with them. My friend shared that when she has done that it was because she was putting her energy into a relationship with one particular person. Not because she was lonely, but because the thought of losing them would really affect her. She did everything for this person. They talked and texted all the time. Then, when he got married, they completely stopped talking. She lost a really good friend.

She shared a poignant analogy: *"And when we stopped talking, it was like a drug. It was like being addicted to a drug and stopping completely, then you go through something like withdrawals. You think about it. It affects you mentally and emotionally, and you feel like you need that drug. It's the same way with [that] person. And, that's how I felt. I felt lonely because I didn't have [his] friendship anymore."*

So, what did she do about this painful loneliness? At first, she cried and asked what she did to deserve this, but finally she got over it. She *"rode it out,"* and *"it went away eventually."* She *"focused on [her] kids more. [She] focused on [herself] more."*

She even focused on the friends she had lost because she had either stopped talking to them or talked to them rarely since she was always focused on and talking to that man. She said that everything worked out. She is even friends with that man again, but not like before.

This is my friend's advice to anyone out there struggling with a similar relationship: *"Just because you dedicate so much time to this person or you see this person one way doesn't mean that they will see you in the same way. So, you need to spread out your love. Have other friends. Have other hobbies. Focus on yourself because you're not lonely. There's a difference in being alone and being lonely, I think."*

Alone. This is what people will do to us. You are trying to find yourself, but you feel weak because every time that you give a hand, people are ready to cut it off. Every time you try to give your heart, someone will take advantage of you. You start to wonder if you ever will find somebody out there you can trust. As you look back when you tried before and were betrayed, you can see that a smile on a face or eyes shining seem to be real, but they were only an illusion. Some of these people are real and some aren't. Real people are like a diamond—a rare and special treasure and once you find them, they become a safe place for you.

Even though there are billions of people on the Earth, there are some people who feel alive in a place of solitude. Yet, have you been out there and seen what mankind is capable of doing? People can come up with a story just to destroy you. Unreal but well designed. And a lot of customers out there are willing to buy that story that will destroy you and finish you. All those lies about you are what people believe. And you are like, *"Man, is there a genuine person who can really read my heart?"* You try to be your own defense attorney, but without experience, it doesn't work. *Who can I hire to go tell the truth? I know myself.* Those lies raise up so high that even you start to believe that those lies about you are real. These things have killed so many people. We see people taking pills or drinking or doing drugs, not because they want to, but because they are seeking this place of solitude. They are seeking a place of security. So, to them, solitude is security because nobody out there in the world understands them. Remember in the chapter *Would You Listen?*, I said that to be able to understand someone, we must do a good job of listening. Since we are not good listeners, we push them out into the middle of nowhere, alone.

Growing up, I would go out and try to play with my brothers. If they would get too rough with me and hurt me, then I would go to my father for help. He would tell me that if I stay in my own corner then no one will come and disturb me. So, I started being in a place of solitude. I would stay by myself in my room and spend hours and hours there. I would come out just for a while, but then I would go back into my room because I felt safe being by myself. Then, it becomes your character. I became introverted and I didn't mind being alone.

You know, a lot of people are not staying on their own just because they want to. You need to understand why. You must understand why they are closing their doors. Something has happened. I can explain about my own experience, but I am sure that every other person who likes the solitude has their own reason. It can be a negative thing, but also, at the same time, it may not be a bad thing. I believe that we should have those moments, but it shouldn't become a lifestyle. As we go along, I will explain how it becomes a lifestyle and what you can do to avoid that. Because, yes, the world out there is not safe, but being alone and not being out there may also be a threat to you because you will not get to experience new things or to know new people or even to enjoy other relationships.

Remember the night that I mentioned in the introduction, there will be moments like these where God might lead you to a place of loneliness in order to speak to your heart. The Bible says in the Book of Hosea *"Therefore, behold, I will allure her, bring her into the wilderness and speak kindly to her,"* and also, in the Book of Deuteronomy, *"Remember how the LORD your God led you all the way in the wilderness these forty years, to humble and test you in order to know what was in your heart, whether or not you would keep his commands. He humbled you, causing you to hunger and then feeding you with manna, which neither you nor your ancestors had known, to teach you that man does not live on bread alone but on every word that comes from the mouth of the LORD."* God takes us to the desert so that He can speak to our hearts.

It's easy sometimes for us to go ahead and condemn people, and say, *"Well, these people don't understand me. There is nobody out there who is willing to listen to me."* Yet, we have so much to say, but people don't have much time to give us. We are not skilled to listen, and we are not very good at it. So, either A) you might have someone who is willing to talk, but not willing to listen. Or, B) you may have people who are willing to listen, but they just don't have much time. Then, on the other hand, you have God who has not only time but eternity to listen to you, and, at the same time, He is always wanting to talk to you. Since you are running here and there, the only way He can do it is to create that moment where you can be alone with Him.

In my first book, *Finding Your Identity: Letting God*

Write Your Unique Story, I wrote a story about when I went on a silent retreat. You know, when I wanted to go on a retreat, I was expecting to go and talk to God, but I found out that the silent retreat was the only one available to me at the time. It was a Catholic retreat, so I met this Sister whose name was Sister McQueen. So, here she was, telling me that even though a lot of people fear being alone, it is not a bad thing.

I listened to her closely because I wanted to understand what she was saying. So, there I was in this retreat and feeling lonely and wanting to experience the presence of God, and this lady was telling me that it was a good thing to be alone.

So, at that point, I can tell you there was some tension, because when someone touches a subject that you don't want to hear, it is going to hurt a little bit. I was thinking, *What is she talking about? She doesn't know! She doesn't understand!* I started having all these things in my heart. It didn't make sense to me until later when I walked out and went to this little wooded area that they had on the property.

So, as I was sitting down, I wanted to pray and started praying, but I would feel God telling me to stay quiet. I wanted to say something, but God was telling me to just to keep quiet and not say a word. So, I really don't have the words to describe that moment of silence, and how peaceful and beautiful it was. I was in nature. I could hear the birds singing and chirping and I could hear the wind blowing and it was so peaceful. I could feel the wind caressing my face. In that very moment of silence, I was able to hear myself and all the struggles that I had and all the questions and all the painful things building up inside of me that I had. Then, I was able to hear God clearly say that He can help, and He can carry that burden. I don't have to fight with it because He will take it. I was at that retreat for three days, but it was at that moment I received my blessing. It was at the place where I was alone. So that is why being alone sometimes is not a bad thing. Finally, I understood what the Sister was talking about.

Here I was a year later, at a time when I was busy with work, ministry, and church. I was running and traveling and planning and doing so much. I was busy Monday to Sunday without a time for a break or time for myself. I would just give and give and give and I was ready to give to others, but nothing was coming in. I found myself with another burden.

You see, we think that when we have that moment with God, then that's it. Sometimes as human beings, we forget. So I forgot what happened. I knew that story and I knew that experience and I knew that encounter, but it was so easy to forget when I got busy that God wanted to talk to me again, but I wasn't there. So, with all the burdens I was carrying from ministry, I was burned out. I had a lot of other things going on, so I was trying to find people to talk to.

I would even call my pastor who was supposed to minister to me, but even in our communication, he would talk to me but I would feel empty. I would try to talk to another person, but they were busy. When I would find someone to talk to me, then I couldn't hear what they said because it was gibberish. I didn't know what they were saying. It's so easy to start blaming people in these moments and say that nobody understands me, nobody wants to listen to me, and nobody loves me. It's so easy, but we don't stop and ask ourselves, who is the man behind the scenes? Maybe it is God who is orchestrating all of this so that you will spend a moment with Him. If no matter where you go for help you are not finding any solutions or comfort or understanding, then maybe God is trying to get you to come to Him.

Remember in the Bible in the Book of Jeremiah, the Prophet Jeremiah was in prison. God came and told him, *"I am the one Who designed these things and I put them together and I executed them."* But Jeremiah was focused on the prison. God said, *"I have this big plan and I want you to talk to Me and I will show you big things no one can tell you about and big things you don't know about."* But Jeremiah was so concerned about the prison.

So, I would find myself at times alone and the loneliness was real. I knew the Word of God, but sometimes at that moment it just felt like it was knowledge but there was no life. Because I went far from the life, which is God—He organized all these things because He wanted to be with me.

As I mentioned in the introduction, I decided to go out for a run just to clear my mind. As I was running out there, I would look at the stars at night and I was just admiring God's creation and I started talking to Him and I told Him that I needed someone I can talk to. I could hear God clearly telling me that, *"I am here,"* and that is all I wanted.

He told me that there are a lot of people out there suffering with these things and they need healing from them, and *"I am here for them, too."* They are sick with wanting people to talk to. God said, *I am here. I have all the time to listen. I have all the time to interact!* He told me that I didn't need to go to another human being to talk to because I had Him. In that 30-minute run, God told me so much. I was so full after that time with God that I had to run into the house and start taking notes. And, God told me to go talk about this subject because there are a lot of people who need My help. *Now, go write about it.*

So, here's the thing that I want you to retain from this chapter: Remember when I told you that my dad told me that if I stay in my corner, then nobody will disturb me? I started staying there for too long of a time, which was a bad thing because you don't want to stay there forever. You still want to come out. But I couldn't go out there in that moment and be with God and see what was wrong in me and maybe that I was the one causing my own problems.

But by being alone, I could see my problems and God could work through me. So, a lot of people will go there and stay forever. You have to go there and allow yourself to be there just for a moment. That is what many people will call a devotion. What you need is to have your own moment with God before you do anything else. It can be at night. It can be at any time. It can be when you are running at the gym. It can be when you are riding to school.

It is your moment with God. It can be anywhere. At the park. It does not have to be a long time. We are all about time, but just give God a minute of your time and that will be fine. God is not in time or space. It does not matter if it is five minutes. It does not matter if it is ten minutes or if it is an hour but find time alone with God. That is where your healing comes from.

When you are alone, do not be prompt to say anything. Stay calm. Allow yourself to be in a time of silence. You can hear what is going on with you and you can see what is wrong with you.

You'll realize that you need help and your help will come from God, and He will come to you and give you a verse that you needed to hear or a devotion that reminds you about who He is.

He will touch us and speak to our hearts in exactly the way we need Him to. We need to feed ourselves up, and realize real food comes from God.

So, do not be afraid. You are not alone. God is with you always.

About Oscar Twikala

*O*scar Twikala graduated from the University of Kinshasa with a degree in international relations. He was born in Lubumbashi, and grew up in Kinshasa, the capital of the DRC (Democratic Republic of the Congo). Oscar moved to the US in 2015. He works as a church planter for IBSA (Illinois Baptist State Association).

Oscar is a pastor in the Gathering of the First Born ministry. Oscar also works full-time as an interpreter, classroom trainer, and recruiter for a food distribution company. Oscar leads The Army of Christ ministry in California. As a servant of Christ, Oscar is passionate about people, which is reflected in the way he devotes his time both day and night to loving, serving, encouraging, discipling, and ministering to everyone he meets. *Alone Yet Not Alone* is Oscar's second book.